A

DESCRIPTION

OF

COCHRANE'S

BINARY LOCOMOTIVE ENGINE,

AND

A DEFENCE OF ITS PRINCIPLES,

IN REPLY TO

ROSS WINANS, ESQ.

AND A REVIEW OF THE WINANS' PATENT FOR THE USE OF DRIVING WHEELS OF LOCOMOTIVES WITH CHILLED CAST IRON FLANGES.

ALSO, AN EXPOSITION OF THE PRINCIPLES OF THE

CONE OF THE WHEEL AND CENTRIFUGAL FORCE,

IN CONNECTION WITH THE PASSAGE OF LOCOMOTIVES THROUGH RAILWAY CURVES.

THE WHOLE FORMING A COMPENDIUM OF VALUABLE INFORMATION NEVER BEFORE PUBLISHED, IN RELATION TO THAT GREATEST ACHIEVEMENT OF MAN, THE RAILWAY SYSTEM.

BY JOHN COCHRANE,

CONSTRUCTING ENGINEER UNION IRON WORKS, BALTIMORE, MD.

BALTIMORE:

PRINTED BY JAMES YOUNG,

Corner of Baltimore and Holliday streets.

1854.

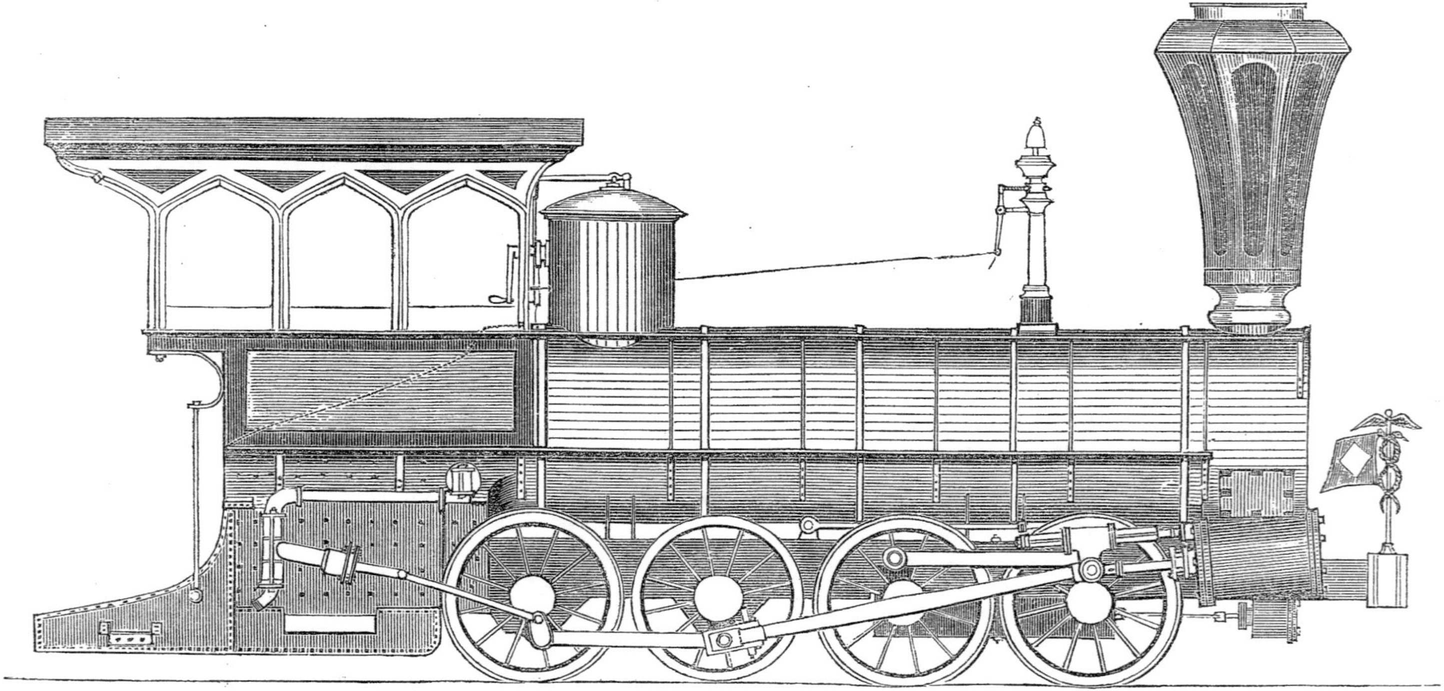

Fig. 1. COCHRANE'S BINARY LOCOMOTIVE ENGINE.

DESCRIPTION

OF THE

BINARY LOCOMOTIVE ENGINE.

While engaged in the employment of the Baltimore and Ohio Railroad Company I had extensive opportunity for observing the practical working of the various forms of locomotive engines in use on that road, and in all, without exception, but especially in those engines which have eight wheels all connected as drivers, the results clearly indicated that there is *ample and urgent necessity for improvement.*

The gradual advancement of the railway system, as a means for the transportation of merchandize, has been followed by a corresponding increase in the size of the locomotives, till, at length, they have attained a weight and power far beyond what was anticipated a few years ago; and this increase in the size of the locomotive, has developed, on a greatly increased ratio, certain inherent evils in its construction; for the gauge of track which was amply sufficient for the small locomotives originally used, proves too contracted for the present large class; thereby causing such a distortion of the original proportions as to materially diminish the necessary firmness and durability of the machine. Hence, in projecting new lines of road for a heavy freight business, the gauge has been increased to five, six and even seven feet, expecting in this way to restore the proper proportions of the machinery.

But whatever be the gauge of the road, the locomotive engine should have within itself the property of *stability*, to ensure efficient performance of duty and the durability of its parts; and of *adaptation*, that it may accommodate itself to the various grades and curves of the road—to the grades by such a cylinder capacity as would prevent the necessity of carrying steam at an excessive pressure on the boiler; and to the curves by a properly arranged truck. And the using of freight locomotives, which have not these essential properties, must be followed by excessive expenses and disasters, as I shall prove in the course of this paper.

In view of the great expense of keeping up the repairs of large freight engines, and the rapid deterioration of the rails on which they run, some eminent engineers have advocated the use of small engines in preference; but expediency determines this question in favor of the largest class. Accordingly I directed my attention to this class, and my investigations have resulted in a radically improved arrangement of the Freight Locomotive, which, from its nature, I denominate the BINARY SYSTEM.

This new mode of construction combines all the economical advantages of the small engines, with power and weight, if required, beyond the capacity of the largest freight engine now in use.

Fig. 1 is a side view of an eight wheeled engine on this principle, drawn to a scale of a quarter inch to the foot. The wheels, all of which are drivers, are of chilled cast iron, 43 inches diameter, and three pairs have flanges. The four front wheels, which are all flanged, are arranged in a truck so that the axles have a radial movement, by means of which the engine can pass with facility around curves as small as sixty feet radius. This truck is attached to the main frame of the engine, in a new and most substantial manner, by means of which no vibratory effect can be imparted to the truck frame by the immediate application of the power to its drivers.

This radiating of the axles of the four front drivers to the curves is one of the most important improvements ever made in the locomotive engine, as it causes it to move in a direction normal to the curve, and to pull as square with the rails in the curves as in the straight parts of the road, *without that abrasive action on the exterior rail,* which is inseparable from the rigid eight wheeled engines, and well known to be destructive to both machinery and rails, and at the same time a great absorbent of the power.

It is generally supposed that the *conicalness* of the wheels is quite sufficient to produce a curvilinear movement of the engine, but it is not so, for this can only be obtained by causing the axles to radiate as described.

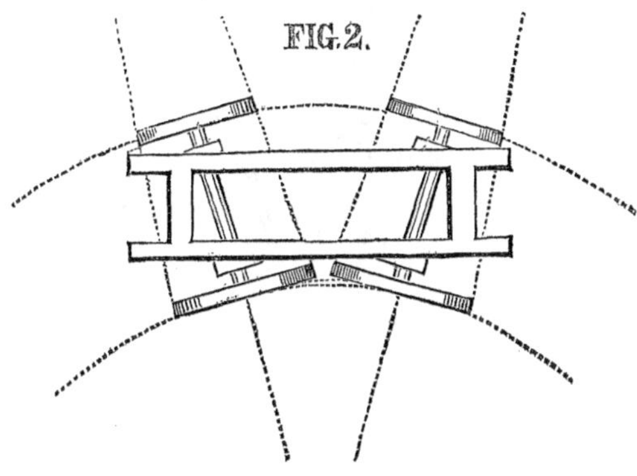

Fig. 2 represents a small experimental wagon which I had constructed to test this question. It has two pairs of wheels, each pair consisting of a large and a small wheel attached to and turning with the axle. The axles were placed in an inclined position to each other, and the large wheels on the convergent side. *The wagon described the arc of a circle against the conical effect of the wheels,* as shown in the diagram, thus conclusively proving that the radiating of the axles is the only correct method for turning curves.

The wheels of the Binary engine may be considered as divided into two sets, viz: Front and Back Drivers, each set being operated by a separate pair of cylinders, making four cylinders in all, as seen in Fig. 3, which is a front elevation of the engine on the same scale as Fig. 1. The pair of cylinders beneath the smoke box operates the truck drivers by means of cranked axles, and the outside pair the back drivers, by means of crank pins in the wheels. Each pair of cylinders with its connections and wheels form a complete system, but is not capable of independent movement, for both systems are so combined together as to secure a simultaneous action in starting, working and stopping, and in all the various manipulations necessary to the management of the engine. This is accomplished by combining the outer and inner cylinder of each side respectively, by means of one steam chest and valve, which produces a perfect unity of action in both systems.

FIG. 3.

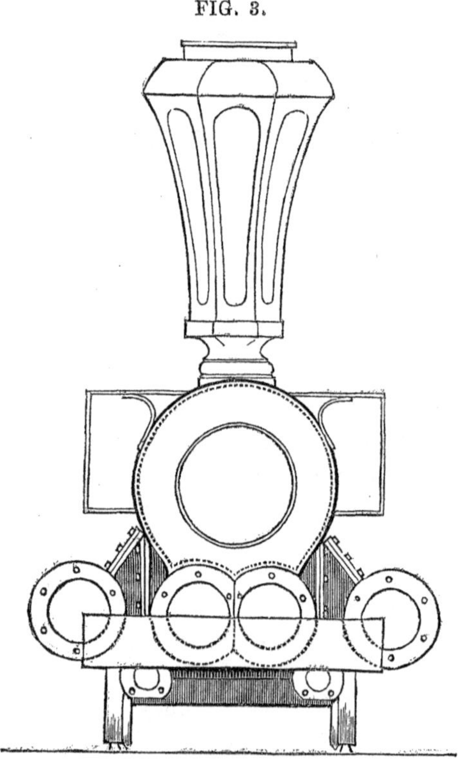

This combination of the cylinders produces a new and important result, for the two cylinders working together, one on each side of each shear of the frame, their forces mutually balance each other, and thus *neutralize that alternate deflecting strain* which cylinders with outside connections exert upon the frame, and which is one of the causes of the very rapid wear and consequent great expense in the repairs of the large freight engines; and, by way of illustration, I would refer to the freight engines of the Baltimore and Ohio Railroad, nearly all of which have cylinders 19 inches bore, or 280 square inches in each piston, which is frequently subjected to a pressure of over 100 lbs. to the square inch, or 28,000 lbs. each, which is further increased as a straining force on the frame, by the leverage of their position, to about 36,000 lbs. Very little constructive skill is required to foresee the ruinous effects on the machinery and frame work of a locomotive by the rapid reciprocating action of this enormous force, compressing and extending the parts alternately with every revolution of the wheels.

This is one of the evils which result from the increased size of the locomotive, but which is completely obviated by the arrangement and combination of the cylinders in the Binary engine; and these cylinders, though small when separately considered, have a greater aggregate capacity than that of the two 19 inch cylinders in the proportion of 100. to 72.3. Therefore, if both engines were required to haul a similar load over the same portions of road, the pressure on their respective boilers would be in the inverse ratio of these numbers; that is, 72.3 lbs. to the square inch in the Binary engine would be equal to 100 lbs. to the square inch in the 19 inch cylinder engine.

Excessive pressure is much more injurious to locomotive than to stationary boilers, from the tremor and jarring to which they are exposed; and the consequence is very apparent in the great leakage of the boilers of these 19 inch cylinder engines; and this is another source of expense in keeping up their repairs, for the tubes and tube sheets soon become cracked from the frequent application of the caulking tools.

The furnace of this engine is also of a highly improved construction, and will burn either Bituminous or Anthracite coal; the fire surface is very large, being five feet six inches wide in the clear. The furnace has two doors, with a water space between them, which in fact forms two chambers, and is of great advantage in the management of the fire.

In the Binary engine the whole weight is available for adhesion, and is distributed equally on the drivers; and in like manner the power is also distributed, first directly to the middle wheels, and from them to the front and back wheels.

It is well known that the sudden impact of a great force on the drivers of a locomotive will make them slip on the rails, and from this cause, when there are four pairs of drivers and the power applied to but one pair, that pair will slip before the power can be transmitted to the others; and thus the tractive foice of the engine is materially diminished at a time when it is most required. But the Binary engine having two sets of main drivers, the impinging force is so extensively distributed, as will, under ordinary circumstances, prevent the slipping of the wheels; and for the same reason the use of sand will in a great degree be dispensed with.

A model of this engine, one fourth of full size, was built for the purpose of illustrating its principles and movement on the rails; and which, at the request of the Board of Managers of the Maryland Institute for the Promotion of the Mechanic Arts, was exhibited at their Fair in October last, and was examined by a large number of engineers from various sections of the Union, who, for the most part, expressed in the strongest terms their admiration of the plan.

This model was also carefully examined by Wm. Parker, Esq., late General Superintendent of the Baltimore and Ohio Railroad, who was so favorably impressed with its general arrangement and capability, that he expressed a desire to have it tried on that road; and for this purpose suggested that application be made through him to the company, and he would lay it before the Board; accordingly an application was presented to him, and on its receipt he instructed the proper officer of the department to which such matters belong, to prepare an estimate for the reconstruction of one of the Winans' geared engines to this plan; but the estimate was not prepared, as Ross Winans, Esq., a builder of locomotives, appeared before the Directors, as I have been credibly informed, and stated to them that his engine required no improvement; that the cone of the wheel gave them ample facility in passing through curves; that the lateral pressure of his engines against the rails is caused by centrifugal force, which is a law of nature, and common to all locomotive engines—that he regarded my plan of engine as a slander on his, and that the very fact of my getting up such an engine is a conclusive proof of my ignorance of these principles—all of which he said he would prove, by models and diagrams to the satisfaction of the most obtuse intellect.

As an engineer, I consider myself called upon to refute these allegations of Mr. Winans, and to defend my improvements in locomotive engines against his opposition; and although I am conscious that he has used his influence against me for his own purposes, and not for the good of the company, I shall assume a higher ground, and endeavor in this defence to promote the public good and the cause of science.

Mr. Winans has been connected with the Baltimore and Ohio Railroad, directly and indirectly, for about 25 years, which gives importance to his opinions respecting railroad matters in the estimation of the directors, who, no doubt, feel safe in adopting his suggestions. But it is possible for Mr Winans to be *mistaken* on the very matters with which he is supposed to be most familiar; and I shall prove by an exposition of the principles of the "cone of the wheel" and of "centrifugal force," that *he is wonderfully mistaken* in these matters; I shall also prove that *he does not understand the principle of his own engine*, and that consequently his opinions in relation to my improvements are of no importance.

A deficiency in the knowledge of constructive science, and of the physical effects of causes in the builders of machinery, is certain to entail pecuniary loss on their patrons; and vast sums are thus wasted to railroad companies by the using of machinery which is not adapted to the peculiarities of their respective roads. To the principles of the cone of the wheel and of centrifugal force are erroneously attributed certain effects on locomotive engines by those who do not understand these matters; it being assumed that the first is a benefit and the other an injury; hence, the real sources of the evils which are associated with the Winans Transportation Engine remain undiscovered by its builder.

His engine *cannot turn curves with the requisite facility, and accordingly it abrades the exterior rail and runs off the track;*

but Mr. Winans alleges that the cone of the wheel gives his engine ample relief in the curves, and that the abrasion of the rails and running off the track are caused by *centrifugal force;* thus attributing to the cone of the wheel advantages which it does not possess, and to centrifugal force evils which it cannot commit, as I shall conclusively prove.

The Cone of the Wheel.

Every one connected with railroads knows that the wheels are the frustums of cones, and almost every one supposes that were it not for this form a locomotive could not move around a curve ; for, say the advocates of this theory, if a *sugar loaf* be rolled on a table, it will describe a circle, of which its apex is the centre.—See Fig. 4.

FIG. 4.

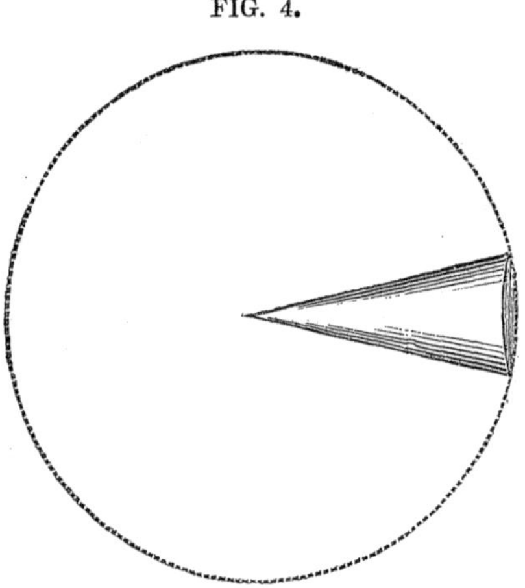

But a single sugar loaf is not a correct illustration of this principle; however, two similar cones placed base to base, as in Fig. 5, will exhibit the exact theoretical principle of a pair of railroad wheels, as laid down by the Chevalier de Pambour, in his Treatise on Locomotives, which is considered a standard work. If this conical spindle, Fig. 5, were supported on the two lines A and B, which are equi-distant from the junction of the two bases, it is very evident that the spindle would roll in a direct or straight course, because the diameters at these lines are equal ; but if the spindle rests on the lines C and D, where the cones are of unequal diameters, the spindle would then roll in a curve, the centre of which would be the apex of a *third cone*, of which the base would be at C, and the inclination of its sides be governed by the diameter at D, as shown by the dotted lines in the diagram.

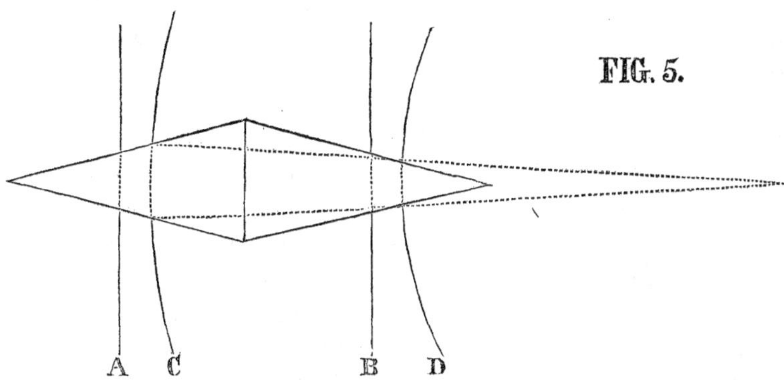

From this illustration it will readily be perceived, that to produce the conical effect, a lateral traverse of the spindle on the bearing points, either way, from the equi-distant position must take place; and that the greater this lateral traverse, the smaller will be the radius of the described curve.

We shall now examine the application of this combined cone principle to a pair of railroad wheels.

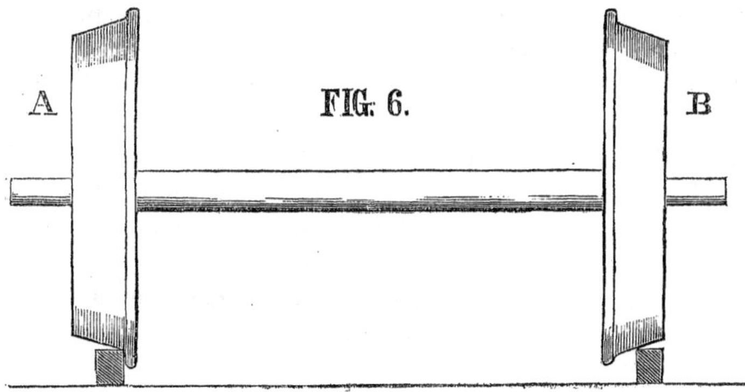

Fig. 6 represents a pair of wheels with their axle and the rails. If both flanges were equi-distant from the rails, the direction of motion would be straight, but as they stand in the diagram, the flange of the wheel A is in contact with one rail, while the flange of the wheel B is at some distance from the other rail; this distance is termed the *play* or *lateral traverse* of the wheels; and the difference in the diameters of the two wheels at the points of bearing on the rails, determines the radius of the curve in which a pair of such wheels will run.

The wheel described by Pambour, page 236, is 3 feet diameter at the interior part or near the flange, and 2 feet 11 inches at the exterior part, its breadth being 3½ inches, and its conical inclination ½ an inch, or $\frac{1}{7}$th of its breadth. And on pages 241, 242, he says: "On a line, the most abrupt curve of which has 500 feet radius, with wagons having wheels of 3 feet diameter, and a play of 1 inch on each side of the way, the equation shows that the least inclination one ought to give the tires is $\frac{1}{12}$; but a more considerable inclination will answer."

Fig. 7 is a full size section of the tire of a Pambour wheel, the lines A and B show the extent of play, which is two inches; and the space between the tire and the line C shows the conical inclination, which is $\frac{1}{7}$th; but the greatest available extent of this inclination, which is limited by the extent of play, is .283 of an inch, consequently the diameter of the wheel is .57 of an inch smaller at the line B than at the line A; and the bearing points of the rails being 58.75 inches apart, a pair of these wheels will describe a curve of 309 feet radius. But by the same mode of calculation a pair of *the Winans' wheels* will describe a curve of 3368 feet radius, which shows there must be a great difference in the conical elements of the two wheels.

Fig. 8 is a full size section of the tire of the Baltimore and Ohio Railroad wheels, and is the precise form of tire used by Mr. Winans in his engines. Similar letters and lines designate the same parts as in Fig. 7. The diameter of the Winans' wheels near the flange is 43 inches, and 3 inches therefrom it is 42¾ inches; the inclination of the tire is $\frac{1}{24}$th, or ⅛th of an inch in 3 inches, and the lateral traverse or play is ¾ of an inch; the greatest extent of difference in their diameters at their limits of play on the rails is $\frac{1}{16}$th of an inch, and the bearing points of the rails are 58.75 inches, as in the Pambour wheels.

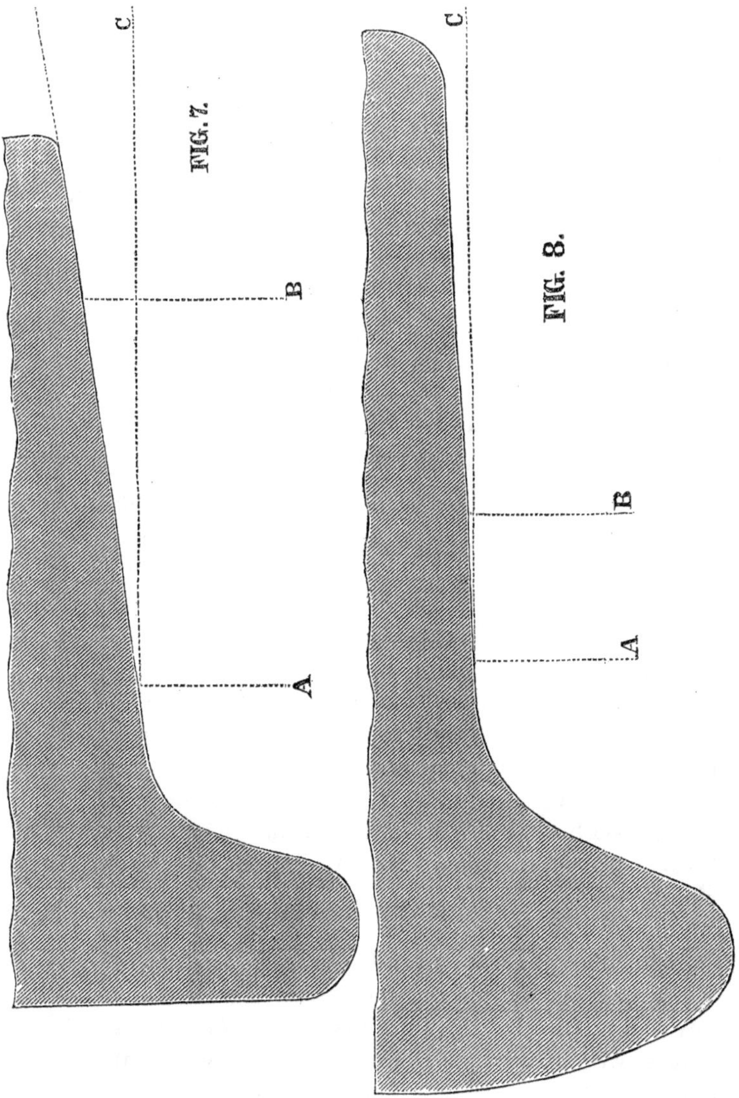

A simple analogical calculation will satisfy any one as to these facts. It is evident that the difference of the diameters at the bearing points of the two wheels, and the distance apart of these bearing points on the rails, determine the angle of convergence; consequently, as often as the major diameter contains the difference of the major and minor diameters, just so many times will the conical radius of the two wheels be greater than the distance apart of their bearing points on the rails. But to make this still plainer we will use the conical elements of the Winans' wheels. The major diameter is 43 inches, the greatest difference of the major and minor diameters $\frac{1}{16}$th of an inch, and the distance apart of the bearing points on the rails 58.75 inches. 43 inches contains $\frac{1}{16}$th of an inch 688 times, and 688 times 58.75 inches are 40,420 inches, or 3368 feet, as before stated.

But as the smallest curve which a pair of the Winans' wheels can describe by rolling on their diameters of greatest conical effect, has a radius of 3368 feet, it is not possible that Mr. Winans ever made these calculations, because, in that case, I presume, he would not have said to the Directors that "the cone of the wheel gave his engines ample facility in passing through the curves;" and if he did make these calculations, then on what authority did he make the above statement? But he can give no authority, for the theory is fallacious, and contrary to mathematical principles, as I shall presently show.

In 1834 the Chevalier de Pambour visited England for the purpose of making a scientific investigation into the railway system of that country, and observing the conical form of wheel in use; he regarded it as a grand principle, and proceeded to deduce general rules for determining this form by calculation; and on page 235 he "shows the differences that must exist between the diameters of the wheels, that the required effect may be obtained." The Chevalier, however, was not a practical man, and therefore could not give the matter that thorough investigation which he otherwise might have done; and this is much to be regretted, for his theories have been adopted almost universally. But if he had examined the *combined effect of two pairs* of these wheels, he would have found to his great surprise that no benefit whatever could be obtained from this form of wheel. And it is singular that this question has not been discussed or noticed in any work on this subject, so far as I am able to ascertain.

Every railway car or engine must have at least two pairs of flanged wheels with parallel axles, which cause the bearing points of the wheels to form a rectangle on the rails, and the rate of convergence being the same for two pairs of wheels as for a single pair, because no change takes place in the convergence of either pair by the combination, therefore, the angle of convergence remaining the same, the distance to the vertex will be increased by the parallel distance of the axles extending the base.

To distinguish these different effects of convergence I will apply the terms *conical radius* to the effect on one pair of wheels, and *convergent radius* to that on two pairs of wheels.

In Fig. 9, A and B represent two pairs of wheels with their axles, but drawn so as merely to exhibit the principles which I wish to explain. In the pair of wheels A, the vertex of their cone is the point C, and D is the vertex of the cone of the wheels B; therefore, C A and D B and the other lines connecting C and D with the small curves are *conical radii*, and by producing the exterior radius of each, they will meet in the point E. Join E A and E B, then will E A and E B be the *convergent radii.*

But I have said that the bearing points of the wheels form a rectangle on the rails, hence the tendency of the car or engine will be as strongly impressed with a direct movement from this cause as by the conical form of the wheels to move in a curve; and, allowing these tendencies to be equal, which they are, very nearly, it is evident that the radii of the curve in which the car or engine will run would lay between the parallels of the axles and the convergent radii. Bisect the angles C A E and E B D formed by the axles and the convergent radii, by the straight lines F A and F B, which meet in the point F, this point is the centre of a curve which is normal to the compound conical effect of two pairs of wheels; and its distance from the curve, which is twice that of the convergent radius, I denominate the *paralactic radius*, because it is intermediate between the centre line of the axles and the convergent radius.

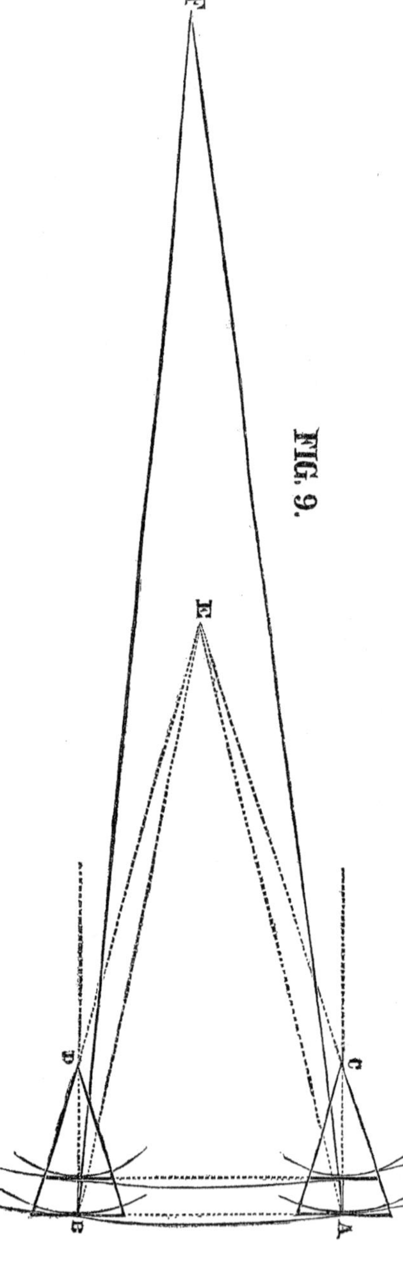

We will now apply these principles to the Winans' engine, the axles of which are 11 feet from centre to centre, and the rate of convergence $\frac{1}{16}$th of an inch in 58.75 inches; therefore, by adding the diameter of one wheel to the central distance of the axles, we will have 175 inches as the base of conical effect, which gives 13,708 feet as the length of the convergent radius, and twice this being the paralactic radius, we have 27,416 feet, or about $5\frac{1}{4}$ miles as the radius of the curve due to the conical effect of the wheels of the Winans' engine!

This requires no comment, so I shall close this article by proving that no benefit whatever, even in the most *attenuated* or *remote degree*, can be obtained from the conical form of the wheel.

In Fig. 9 it will be observed that the straight line which connects the bearing points of the two interior wheels falls within the curve, and is in fact the chord of the intercepted arc; therefore, the interior back wheel must roll towards the interior rail; and as the straight line which connects the bearing points of the exterior wheels also falls within the curve, the exterior front wheel will therefore roll towards the outside rail; both of these wheels, that is, the outer front wheel and the inner back wheel, will have the largest parts of their diameters on the rails, while their opposite wheels will have the smallest parts of their diameters, according to the play of the wheels, on the rails at the same time; that is, the conical effects of the two pairs of wheels are thrown in opposite directions, which completely neutralize each other, or simply producing no other effect than what is obtained by wheels of a truly cylindrical form of tire.

Centrifugal Force.

We will now consider the operation of centrifugal force in railway curves, in which matter, also, the Chevalier de Pambour is a standard authority. On page 237 of his work he says, "Let us suppose that the velocity of the motion be 20 miles per hour, and the radius of the curve 500 feet; in that case the centrifugal force will be $\frac{1}{19}$th part of the weight of the body in motion." And on page 238 he says, "The effort of this force exerting itself in the direction of the radius will be to push all the wagons out of the curve. If the two sides of the railway are of equal elevation the wagons will be stopped in this lateral motion only by the flange of the wheel against the rail. But if we give to the outward rail a surplus of elevation above the inward one, it is clear that in increasing sufficiently that elevation, we shall be able to master at last the centrifugal force in such a manner as to permit it only to produce just the displacing we want. In fact, by raising in that manner the outward side, we will change the railway into an inclined plane. The wagons placed on that plane ought, by virtue of their gravity, to slip towards the lower rail. On the other hand, the centrifugal force pushes them against the outward rail, which is the highest We create, then, by that means, a counterpoise to the centrifugal force." And on this principle he gives, on page 243, the height of the exterior rail to be 2.83 inches, as necessary to a curve of 500 feet radius, and a speed of 20 miles per hour.

From these quotations it is evident that PAMBOUR predicates his theory on the abstract supposition that *the wagons are free to slip laterally on the rails by the most trifling degree of force that may be applied to them*, and that consequently *centrifugal force* would cause the wagons to *slide off the rails*, were it not for "the flange of the wheel." This force he accordingly balances by bringing into play the action of *gravitation;* also, in an abstract sense, by elevating the exterior rail to the required angle, so as to produce a *counterpoise* to the centrifugal force.—Thus, in a curve of 500 feet radius, and the speed of the wagons 20 miles per hour, the centrifugal force will be equal to the $\frac{1}{19}$th part of the adhering weight, and is counter-balanced by elevating the exterior rail of the curve 2.83 inches, which is equal to a grade of 254 feet to the mile, and makes an angle to the horizon of 2 deg., 53 min.

But the Chevalier de Pambour ought to have recollected that on page 252 he shows, and that correctly, the force of adhesion to be $\frac{1}{6}$th of the adhering weight; therefore, a wagon will not slip until a greater force than $\frac{1}{6}$th of its own weight is applied to it; and consequently it is totally impossible that a centrifugal force of only $\frac{1}{19}$th the weight of that wagon could make it slide across the rails.

Again, he elevates the exterior rail in this case to an angle of 2 deg., 53 min., and intimates that that angle will cause the force of gravity to slide the wagon down towards the interior rail; but he should have known *that bodies will not slip down an inclined plane till its elevation exceeds the limiting angle of repose*, which for iron on iron is about 10 deg. Therefore, it cannot be possible that gravity will cause a wagon to slide across the rails at an angle of only 2 deg., 53 min.

From this brief exposition of principles and facts every one will readily understand that neither gravity nor centrifugal force can exercise any sliding effect on a Winans' engine; but it must be observed that these engines seldom move faster through a curve of 500 feet radius than 10 miles per hour, at which speed the centrifugal force is only one-fourth of what it is at 20 miles per hour; because its decrease is as the *square root* of the velocity, and the $\frac{1}{4}$th of $\frac{1}{19}$ is equal to but $\frac{1}{76}$th part of the adhering weight. Here again we might ask with surprise, does Mr. Winans know this? and if so, how came he to attribute the lateral pressure of his engines to centrifugal force, when in the nature of things it is not possible that this property of the Winans' engine can in any way be associated with centrifugal force! Therefore it must have its origin in the *construction* of the engine, a fact which I shall prove in its proper place.

When the Chevalier de Pambour visited the Liverpool and Manchester Railroad, he observed that "the outer rails of the curves were elevated a little above the interior rails," which elevation, he says, was arrived at "*only by approximation*," and on page 243 he gives "a practical table of the surplus of elevation to be given to the outward rails in the curves, in order to annul the retarding effect of the curves."

In my opinion he totally mistook the object which the English engineers had in view in so constructing their curves; had the *centre of gravity* of their "wagons" and locomotives been near the rails, no such "surplus of elevation" would have been required, but the centre of gravity being, in most cases, about 4 feet above the rails, where centrifugal force does act by *causing the wheels of the exterior side to press with additional force on the rail*, and the interior wheels with less force; the exterior rails were accordingly elevated so as to cause the centre of gravity to *lean against* the centrifugal force, and thus equalize the pressure on both rails.

This principle is perfectly illustrated by a horse when galloping in a circus, the *quicker* he moves, the *greater* will be the pressure of centrifugal force, and to resist it, the greater will be his angle of inclination; because his centre of gravity is also considerably above the ground; and if the circle in which he runs be examined, it will be found elevated towards the outer edge, in order that the *feet* of the animal may bear *equally and square* upon its surface. But while the horse, by his natural instinct, selects the proper grade of elevation to suit his velocity, the fixed railway curve must serve for all speeds, and its inclination can, therefore, only be determined by "*approximation*," as the circumstances of speed, weight, travel and transportation may decide. A little elevation is a benefit, but if the approximate angle be much exceeded, it will produce a very injurious effect.

According to the Pambour theory, the inclination as given in his practical table, page 243, will prevent the flanges of the wheels from coming into contact with the exterior rail of the curves; for instance, in curves of 1000 feet radius he assigns for the surplus of elevation 1.43 inches; but *in practice* this elevation *will not* prevent the contact of the flange with the exterior rail; hence, a little more is given, and that not producing any sensible effect, they keep on adding to the height; but still the abrasion goes on, even after $6\frac{3}{4}$ inches have been tried on a curve of this radius! as I have found by the application of the spirit level. Now, if these matters were properly understood, no such "surplus of elevation" as this would be pointed out as a triumph of modern skill in the construction of railroads for facilitating the passage of the curves.

The centrifugal force of a Winans' engine in a curve of 1000 feet radius, at 10 miles per hour, is about $\frac{1}{154}$th part of its weight, equal to 376 lbs.; therefore, if the rails were of the same height, the pressure on the exterior rail would be about 376 lbs. more than on the interior rail, which would be a matter of trivial consequence; but the elevation of the exterior rail to a little over 6 inches, throws the centre of gravity of the engine vertically over a point 5 inches out of centre towards the interior rail, causing the engine to bear on that rail with the weight of about 34,000 lbs., and on the exterior rail with only about 24,000 lbs., making an excess of 10,000 lbs. pressure on the interior rail in the attempt to form an equipoise by means of gravity!

Thus, a surplus of elevation is given to the exterior rail of over 6 inches, or an inclination equal to about 540 feet to the mile; that a centrifugal force of 376 lbs. may not push an engine weighing 58,000 lbs. up this inclined plane against the exterior rail!

From this malconstruction of the curves, engines of 58,000 lbs. weight are made to press the interior rails with as much force as though they weighed 68,000 lbs. each!

If any one will examine the curves of a railway, a marked difference may be noticed in the two rails, where this excessive surplus of elevation has been adopted, and it will be found, that although the *inner edge* of the exterior rail may be abraded considerably by the action of the flange, its upper surface for the most part is good and solid, while the surface of the interior rail, on the other hand, has a crushed and loose appearance, as if made of inferior iron, presenting, in fact, the contrast that might be expected in two roads of equal travel, one using engines of 48,000 lbs. weight, and the other engines of 68,000 lbs. for the deterioration of the rails, from the crushing effects of heavy engines, increases much more rapidly than what appears to be due to the mere increase of weight after a certain limit is exceeded.

This specimen of engineering is worthy the notice of those interested, for without producing the *least prevention* of contact of the flange and rail, it fully confirms the suggestion that if the approximate angle be much exceeded, injurious effects must ensue.

From this exposition it is evident that *centrifugal force* exerts a *vertical* pressure on the exterior rails in curves, instead of a lateral pressure, as asserted by Mr. Winans, and indeed most generally believed by practical men; and by those also who are not practical, but who undertake to give abstractions in science, as practical rules by which millions have been expended to no purpose.

Having demonstrated that the lateral pressure of the Winans' engine against the rails is not caused by centrifugal force, I shall now prove that it is the natural result of the defective principles on which these engines are constructed. The axles of these engines, Mr. Winans says, in his specification, "are placed permanently parallel to each other;" this controls the tendency of their movement to a direct or straight course, and thus renders them unsuitable for curved roads, such as the Baltimore and Ohio Railroad. But that they may be used on this or any other road having curves, Mr. Winans was obliged to abandon the mode which he says in his said specification that he *prefers*, and was compelled to adopt another mode, which, for good reasons, he did not prefer; but none of his modes answer the purpose which he has specified, viz: to turn curves with the requisite facility. Accordingly, it is in the *curves* that the defective principles of his engines are most apparent, by the manner in which they scale off the edge of the rails, and by running off the track; but when it is considered that the front guiding flange is a secant to the curve, and in abrasive contact with the rail, we can readily perceive that a very small obstacle, such as would in no wise obstruct a truck engine, is amply sufficient to throw a Winans' engine from the track.

The mode which Mr. Winans adopts to enable his engines to pass through the curves is to make the four middle wheels without flanges; the effect of which is most disastrous, as it permits the momentum of the engine to concentrate in a single point where the flange of the front wheel impinges the exterior rail, causing such percussions as frequently displace the rails and break the flanges of the wheels, and is the true cause of the many accidents which result from the use of these engines, abundantly proving them to be most uncertain and unsafe in their operations; and they have in consequence killed more people, destroyed more property, and caused more detention to travel on the road, than any form of locomotive engine ever built, in proportion to their number and time in use. And the expense to the Baltimore and Ohio Railroad Company for extra repairs and losses traceable to the use of these engines amounts annually to an immense sum.

These engines not only consume a large portion of the proceeds of this road, but they *depreciate its character for safety and the speedy conveyance of passengers*, and although they are not passenger engines, they interfere with the travel of the road, which is the most profitable part of the business, causing it to fall far below the reasonable expectation of the company, by the frequency of the accidents to which they are so liable.

I will now notice the TRACTIVE CAPACITY of the Winans' engine. This engine has indeed eight wheels, all connected as drivers, but owing to the defective transmission of the power to its front pair of wheels, its tractive capacity is not beyond what is due to the adhesion of six of its drivers; and consequently it must carry as *dead weight*, the 14,500 lbs. which rest on the two front wheels; leaving but 33,500 lbs. for adhesion, which reduces its force 25 per cent.

Now it is evident that every pound in the weight of a locomotive engine which is not available for adhesion, is equal to the transportation of so much freight *without compensation;* and this dead weight must be carried through every curve and up every grade, in which latter case it often forms the seventeenth part of the load. As this dead freight must occasion *some* loss to the company, if any one will take the trouble of computing the amount of this loss in a year's service of one hundred of these dead weight engines, he will obtain a result which may probably astonish him.

In comparing the Binary engine with the Winans' engine, we observe—

1st. Every pound of its weight is useful for adhesion, and its weight being 60,000 lbs., its tractive capacity is to that of the Winans' engine as 600 is to 335.

2dly. The Binary engine cannot leave the track, except from the intervention of extraordinary causes; when, from the principles of its construction, the Winans' engine will leave the track from causes of so trifling a character as could be passed over by a truck locomotive in perfect safety.

3dly. The Binary engine will pass through curves of 60 feet radius with facility, while the Winans' engine does not possess a single mechanical expedient by means of which it can pass through curves of any radius with facility.

The Winans' Patent.

Mr. Winans is generally supposed to be the *inventor* of locomotive engines with six or eight driving wheels. This is by no means the case. His claim relative to the wheels is merely for the use of chilled cast iron flanches in combination with an engine having six or eight driving wheels with axles parallel to each other. He procured a patent for this idea on the 14th of October, 1846, and his specification is now on file in the patent office, signed by himself and witnessed by John H. B. Latrobe and Edwin L. Brundage.

The writer of this specification was evidently more skilled in law than in mechanics, for it is, perhaps, the most subtle document that was ever imposed on the patent office, and at the same time one of the boldest attempts, by assumption, to grasp a fortune from the railroad companies of the Union that was ever perpetrated.

Mr. Winans does not claim the use of any number of driving wheels or bearing points on the rails; but his claim is for the use in a locomotive engine of six or more driving wheels made of a *certain material,* on the representation that although four such wheels had been used, *a new and important result* arises from the use of six or more of them! The following paragraph, which I here give verbatim from his specification, contains a complete synopsis of the case. After describing various modes for permitting an engine with six or eight driving wheels to pass through curves, *all of which devices,* however, he very candidly admits *were the inventions of other persons,* he says: "*By combining with the said devices* THE USE OF CHILLED CAST IRON FLANCHES, *a new and original combination is obtained,* and the *difficulty of using six or eight driving wheels with their axles parallel to each other* WILL BE OBVIATED, WITHOUT DANGER FROM RUNNING OFF THE TRACK, AND WITH THE REQUISITE FACILITY OF PASSING THROUGH CURVES AND TURN-OUTS, *as I* (Ross Winans) *have experimentally ascertained.*"

If this *combination* gave the "*requisite facility* of passing through curves and turn-outs," prior to the date of the patent, "*without danger from running off the track,*" it will do so *now,* and there being NO DANGER, *there is no* POSSIBILITY *of running off the track.*

But Mr. Winans having ascertained, by actual experience on the Baltimore & Ohio and other railroads, *that this combination* will NOT *obviate the said difficulty* without danger of running off the track, and that it will NOT *give the requisite facility* of passing through curves and turn-outs; he, therefore, *now* says, that *this difficulty is caused by* CENTRIFUGAL FORCE! and to prove that this is really the case, he has had a "curiously contrived" *flexable curve* constructed on the Locust Point branch of the Baltimore and Ohio railroad, by which, I am informed, he has "experimentally ascertained" to his entire satisfaction that he is right in this conjecture. He says "this force is *a law of nature*," it must therefore have been in *full operation* at the time he proved the utility and advantage of "*this new and original combination*," as he terms it. If "*this law of nature*" *now* deprives this "combination" of the *utility* which he has *claimed* for it, *it could never have had this utility*, *consequently* IT WAS NOT ENTITLED TO A PATENT; and Mr. Winans having *procured* this patent *through representations which he knows to be erroneous*, IT IS UNQUESTIONABLY INVALID.

Chilled cast iron driving wheels have been in use on the Baltimore and Ohio Railroad for about 20 years past, and it was and still is customary on this road to replace the worn out wrought iron tires of the engines, which have been purchased by the company, with wheels of chilled cast iron; and when the increase of business would have required, engines with six or eight driving wheels, (as had been introduced on other roads) *such wheels would inevitably have been made of chilled cast iron;*—a fact well known to Mr. Winans, and he also well knew that a large number of such engines would be required by this company to meet the increase of business by the extension of the road; he, therefore, "secured to himself and legal representatives, by letters patent, the right to make and use" *chilled cast iron wheels for all engines requiring more than four drivers*, on the *pretext* that he had *discovered* and *experimentally ascertained* that when *more than four* chilled cast iron driving wheels were used in one engine, *a new and original combination was obtained!* WHEN IN FACT NO NEW PROPERTY WAS IMPARTED TO THE WHEELS BY THIS COMBINATION; thus obliging the company to depart from their established custom of using driving wheels of chilled cast iron, (for the making of which they had large facilities) or pay him for the privilege of using them!

Mr. Winans alleges, in another part of his specification that the *advantage* of his "new combination" "*is valuable and important* in proportion as the distance between the front and hind axles of an engine having its axles parallel *is increased*."

This is a palpable misrepresentation, being a substitution of the *necessity* of relief for the *means* of relief. The longer the chord of a given arc, the longer will be its versed sine; and consequently, on this principle, *the greater the distance apart of the front and back wheels of a locomotive, the greater will be its difficulty in passing through curves;* hence, *the greater this distance the greater the necessity* of some means of relief; but this difficulty is not met with the requisite facility by this "combination" of Mr. Winans, as the ingenious wording of his specification would lead one to suppose.

The mere extending of the space between the axles, however, is not the subject of a patent; four wheeled engines have been built in which the parallel distance of the axles was *sixteen feet;* five feet more than the extreme distance of the eight wheeled engines of Mr. Winans! and yet these four wheeled engines derived no valuable or important advantage by this extension of their wheels.

Whatever advantage is possessed by driving wheels with flanges of chilled cast iron, was realized as perfectly in the engines built by Phineas Davis, for the Baltimore and Ohio Railroad, twelve years before the date of the Winans' patent, as it ever has been since. It is the *back and front wheels* alone of the Winans' engine which are flanged, and on them depends the keeping of the engine on the track; *the middle wheels are without flanges,* and therefore cannot assist in anywise to facilitate the passage of the curves, or to obviate the danger of running off the track. How preposterous then for Mr. Winans to expatiate, in his specification, on the advantages of the "*chilled cast iron flanch,*" when he has not added a single "*flanch*" to the engine! *nor combined therewith a single element by which additional facility or safety is imparted to a locomotive in passing through curves!* much less to give it the "requisite facility" "without danger from running off the track!!" Consequently, Mr. Winans has not, nor ever had any right, to exact money from any party by virtue of this patent.

The seal of the patent office cannot be appropriated to the protection of a mere *combiner of other men's devices,* so that he may extort funds from the public for the use of a combination which he knows to be inoperative through "a law of nature" or by any other cause. The discovery of a mere abstract principle, resting in theory and speculation, but *of no utility*, as in this case, is not the subject of a patent; and the granting or *procuring* of a patent in such a case, by any means, is contrary to the spirit and intention of the patent law, and is without the pale of its protection.

Six and eight wheeled engines, with chilled cast iron drivers, are now being extensively used on various railroads without acknowledging the right of Mr. Winans, except the Baltimore & Ohio and a few others, which pay him his demands. It is a fact well understood that these wheels with parallel axles cannot be made to keep the track in curves, with any certainty, but as they are cheap and convenient to manufacture, they are pretty generally used, without any idea of realizing the advantages claimed by Mr. Winans in his patent. Now, to sustain this patent Mr. Winans must prove, that, by "the use of wheels with flanches of chilled cast iron," in combination with the devices enumerated by him, "*the difficulty of using six or eight driving wheels with their axles parallel to each other,*" IS "OBVIATED *without danger from running off the track, and with the requisite facility of passing through* CURVES *and turn-outs,*" according to his specification, WHICH IS ABSOLUTELY IMPOSSIBLE for him to do; therefore, his said patent is null and void in law.

The opposition of Mr. Winans to my improvements in locomotive engines, and his misrepresentations in the matter, have compelled me to give a description of the Binary engine, and to defend its principles, that the utility and necessity of these improvements might be understood by the community; and to do this with proper effect I was obliged to exhibit the construction of the engine of Mr. Winans and review his patent, and also to dissipate the false theories of the cone of the wheel and centrifugal force in connection with locomotive engines.

Although these erroneous theories commenced with the railway system itself, and have been established and confirmed for some 20 years by men of high attainments in science, but evidently destitute of practical knowledge and experience; and have been adopted and tenaciously adhered to by Mr. Winans without investigation, I have so completely and incontrovertibly cleared them away by the sound principles of mathematical science, that surprise will be excited that they ever became so generally adopted, or continued so long unchallenged. And having done this, and also having proved that the Binary engine is predicated on true principles, as elicited by a careful and thorough investigation of the whole matter, I think that I cannot be charged with presumption in asserting that the Binary engine will come fairly up to all that I claim for it.

While quietly pursuing these investigations, and constructing the model of a locomotive which would perform what is erroneously attributed to the cone of the wheel, and that would be clear of the evils which are charged without cause to centrifugal force, I little expected that this model, the exponent of my views, should be referred to by *Mr. Winans* as a most conclusive evidence of my ignorance in these very matters, in order that he might prevent thereby the introduction of my improvements.

It cannot be expected that the directors of railroad companies should be so skilled in all the ramifications of mathematical and mechanical science as to be able to detect false theories in relation to the construction of locomotive engines, or the working of a railroad ; but they are not to be deceived on that account. Let Mr. Winans now come forward with his long promised "models and diagrams" with which he was to "convince the most *obtuse intellect*" that he was right in the assertions he advanced to the directors in relation to his engine and the principles of mine, and controvert my statements as herein set forth, if he can; for he is bound in duty to the Baltimore and Ohio Railroad Company, and to this community, either to do this or to acknowledge his total misapprehension of these matters.

In the mean time I invite particular attention to the within diagram, Fig. 8, of the tire of the Winans' wheel; observe the minute fraction of the cone represented between the face of the tire and the line C, between A and B, which is the full extent of the inclination of the cone on which Mr. Winans depends for *ample relief* to his engines in curves. And let the *patent* of Mr. Winans and the common theories of *the cone of the wheel* and *centrifugal force* be also carefully considered, and I feel confident that every man of *intelligence* will be convinced of their perfect absurdity, and that they cannot fail to perceive that a great responsibility rests on Mr. Winans by his influencing the directors against the introduction of improvements in locomotive engines, which would promote the security of life and property on railroads, and reduce the running expenses; for any such improvement, according to the principles of political economy, is A BENEFIT TO EVERY INDIVIDUAL.

The BINARY ENGINE was designed to overcome the natural difficulties in the curves and undulations of the Baltimore and Ohio Railroad, and to enable that road to compete with those of more favorable alignment and grade; and it is better adapted to accomplish this purpose than any other locomotive yet produced; and when tried it will be found that were all the Winans' engines (exclusive of the geared engines) which are now on this road, altered to this plan, which they can be, their tractive capacity would be increased 25 per cent., which would be equivalent to 25 new engines, worth about $250 000; and that the whole cost of reconstruction would be paid in one year's use, from the reduction alone in the expenses for repairs of locomotives, road and rails, passenger, burden and coal cars, and losses from accidents, which amounted in the aggregate last year to $659,140.06, as per company's last annual report, page 37.

I respectfully submit the question to the President, Directors and Stockholders of this road, and all who are interested in its prosperity and that of the city of Baltimore—is it proper or consistent with the spirit of enterprise and progress that an engine with the properties which I have demonstrated the Binary engine to possess, should be put down; and that this road, the great and increasing business of which meriting the most perfect form of engine that can be procured, must be debarred of its use, through the influence of Mr. Winans, lest its adoption might interfere with his own pecuniary interests?

JOHN COCHRANE.

APPENDIX.

When the foregoing had passed through the press, I observed that two unimportant words had been omitted on page 26, in that paragraph of the specification of Mr. Winans' patent, which I professed to give verbatum; the words "wheels with" were unintentionally left out in preparing the manuscript, without, however, impairing the sense; but to prevent any one from saying that I gave an incorrect statement of the said specification, I herewith append a true copy of it entire, which, the reader will perceive, fully confirms and establishes all that I have said in relation to it.

J. C.

TO ALL WHOM IT MAY CONCERN.—Be it known that I, Ross Winans, of the city of Baltimore, in the State of Maryland, Civil Engineer, have made an improvement in the manner of constructing Locomotive Steam Engines to be used on railroads, with six or eight driving wheels, and I do hereby declare that the following is a full and exact description thereof:

In the combination and arrangement of some of its parts, my improved Locomotive Steam Engine resembles one that was built by Mr. Hopkins Thomas, with the six driving wheels, and which was used on the Beaver Meadow railroad; but his engine was found to be objectionable on account of its two great tendency to run off the road; to obviate which, and to increase the number of driving wheels and points of bearing on the rail from four to six or eight, are among the objects of my improvement.

In the accompanying drawings I have represented my improved engine under two different modifications or modes of construction. Fig. 1 is an engine with six wheels, all of which are driving wheels, two pair of driving wheels being in front of and one pair behind the fire box. Fig. 2 is a similar engine with all the driving wheels before the fire box. Fig. 3 is an engine with eight wheels, all of which are driving wheels, with the cylinders in an inclined position. Fig. 4 is a similar engine drawn to a larger scale, with the cylinders in an horizontal position, which position is preferred.

The motive power from the steam cylinder A (in the accompanying drawings) is communicated directly to the pair of driving wheels B, by means of connecting rods C, operating on crank pins on one pair of the said driving wheels, or on cranks on their axles; the connecting rods D D operating upon cranks on the other axles in a manner well understood, so as to make all six or eight wheels driving wheels. The axles of the respective pairs of wheels are placed permanently parallel to each other, and to enable the wheels to arrange themselves in a position to pass readily around curves on the road, or through switches, a lateral or end play is allowed the axles when all the wheels are furnished with flanches. This lateral play of the axles and wheels may be obtained in various ways, but the mode which I prefer is to make the journals of the axles longer than the boxes in which they run, so as to allow of the requisite end play, or the boxes may be allowed to play laterally for this purpose. To enable an engine with six or eight wheels, and all the axles parallel to each other, to run with facility upon curves of short radius, and through switches, one of the two following devices may be allowed: first, a lateral play of about an inch to each axle may be allowed, or double that play on the middle axle or axles if the end ones have only the usual play; or secondly, this lateral or end play may be dispensed with, and the capacity of adaptation be still retained by forming the middle pair or pairs of wheels without flanches. To equalize the pressure on the respective driving wheels, and consequently to distribute the weight or bearing of the locomotive on the rails on six or eight points, and the better to preserve the proper distribution of the weight on each of the wheels when passing over the uneven parts of the road, a vibrating spring, such as is shown at a a in the respective drawings may be used. This vibrating spring turns on a fulcrum b below its centre, and the rods c c bear on its ends and upon the upper boxes of the two contiguous driving wheels. A device analagous to this, consisting of a vibrating lever and spring, has been used by Messrs. Eastwick & Harrison on a locomotive engine, for which they obtained letters patent. A similar device was also used by Mr. Hopkins Thomas. The axles of the respective pairs of wheels of Mr. Thomas' engine were also arranged permanently to each other, and lateral play was allowed to the axles and wheels as herein described, for the purpose of promoting the easy passage through curves and turn-outs, and the steam power was transmitted from the cylinder to the respective driving wheels by means of cranks and connecting rods, as herein described. The above devices mentioned as having been used by Mr. Hopkins Thomas, I do not consider as new, either taken individually or in their combination with each other, they having been used and combined with each other, as above remarked, by that gentleman, in the construction of an engine with six propelling wheels, but without producing thereby a machine possessing the advantages obtained by my improvement, or capable of passing through the curves and turn-outs of the road with the requisite ease, facility and safety. By combining with the said devices the use of wheels with flanches of chilled cast iron, a new and original combination is obtained, and the difficulty of using six or eight driving wheels with their axles parallel to each other will be obviated without danger from running off the track, and with the requisite facility of passing through curves and turn-outs, as I have experimentally ascertained. With the ordinary driving wheels with wrought iron flanches this would not be the case. I do not intend to claim the use of driving wheels for engines with flanches of chilled cast iron as new, when taken alone, but wheels with chilled cast iron flanches are an element, which, when combined with the other devices enumerated, or with devices substantially the same, and with six or eight driving wheels, forms a new combination, which is a new and useful improvement. Chilled cast iron flanches to the wheels which guide an engine on the track promote a more easy and safe transit through curves and turn-outs, and along the entire road, than would be the case were wheels with wrought iron flanches used; an advantage which is valuable and important in proportion as the distance between the front and hind axles of an engine is increased. The extreme hardness of the chilled cast iron flanch causes it to preserve its original and proper shape much better than a wrought iron flanch. This better preservation of the form, together with the extreme hardness and the smoothness of the chilled cast iron flanches, ensure their gliding off the rails, instead of mounting them, and the engine is thereby guided along the track with greater safety and with less resistance to the moving power than could be done by wheels having wrought iron flanches, all other things being equal. Having thus fully set forth the nature of my improvement, WHAT I CLAIM and desire to be secured by letters patent is the employment of wheels with chilled cast iron flanches, in combination with an engine having six or eight driving wheels, with axles parallel to each other, and accommodating itself to curves and turn-outs, by any of the devices or modes herein described for that purpose, and having the power applied to all the axles by connecting rods and cranks.

ROSS WINANS.

Witnesses:

JNO. H. B. LATROBE,
EDWIN L. BRUNDAGE.

Exd. L. S.

Patented 14*th of October*, 1846.

www.ingramcontent.com/pod-product-compliance
Lightning Source LLC
LaVergne TN
LVHW011121110826
845150LV00008B/2217

* 9 7 8 1 4 1 8 1 9 5 6 2 5 *